WILDCATS

Clouded Leopards

by Jennifer L. Marks

Consulting Editor: Gail Saunders-Smith, PhD

Consultant: Robin Keith
Senior Research Coordinator
San Diego Zoo's Institute for Conservation Research

CAPSTONE PRESS
a capstone imprint

Pebble Plus is published by Capstone Press,
151 Good Counsel Drive, P.O. Box 669, Mankato, Minnesota 56002.
www.capstonepub.com

032010
005740CGF10

 Books published by Capstone Press are manufactured with paper
containing at least 10 percent post-consumer waste.

Library of Congress Cataloging-in-Publication Data
Marks, Jennifer, 1979–
     Clouded leopards / by Jennifer L. Marks.
     p. cm.—(Pebble plus. Wildcats)
     Includes bibliographical references and index.
     Summary: "Simple text and full-color photos explain the habitat, life cycle, range, and behavior of clouded
leopards"—Provided by publisher.
     ISBN 978-1-4296-4482-2 (library binding)
     1. Clouded leopard—Juvenile literature. I. Title. II. Series.
QL737.C23M2745 2011
599.75—dc22   2010002797

Editorial Credits
Katy Kudela, editor; Bobbie Nuytten, designer; Svetlana Zhurkin, media researcher; Eric Manske, production specialist

Photo Credits
Alamy/Dan Bachmann, 16–17; First Light, 13
Corbis/Tom Brakefield, 19
Getty Images/The Image Bank/Art Wolfe, 7
Photoshot/Bruce Coleman/Erwin & Peggy Bauer, cover; Bruce Coleman/Lynn M. Stone, 9
Shutterstock/Andy Poole, 1, 15; Chris Lorenz, back cover, 5; Fenton (paw prints), cover and throughout;
     Glen Gaffney, 11; Michael D. Skelton, 21

The author dedicates this book to Trudi and Elliot, her favorite felines.

Note to Parents and Teachers

The Wildcats series supports national science standards related to life science. This book
describes and illustrates clouded leopards. The images support early readers in understanding
the text. The repetition of words and phrases helps early readers learn new words. This book
also introduces early readers to subject-specific vocabulary words, which are defined in the
Glossary section. Early readers may need assistance to read some words and to use the Table of
Contents, Glossary, Read More, Internet Sites, and Index sections of the book.

Table of Contents

Hard to Spot

Deep in the forest,

a clouded leopard

spies its prey.

The wildcat creeps closer.

Then, pounce!

Clouded leopards live in
southeast Asia's forests
and rain forests.
These shy cats stay hidden
in the wilderness.

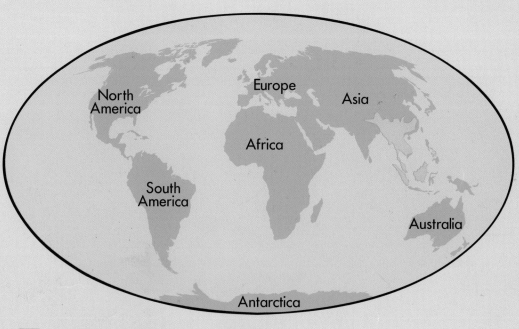

☐ **where clouded leopards live**

Clouded Leopard Bodies

Clouded leopards are
small but strong.
They weigh up to
50 pounds (23 kilograms).

house cat

clouded leopard

Clouded leopards are

good tree climbers.

Their powerful legs

and wide paws

help them dart up or down.

In trees or on the ground,

clouded leopards

are hard to see.

Their spotted fur blends in

with plants and shadows.

Skilled Hunters

Clouded leopards hunt on
the ground and in trees.
They use their long fangs
and strong jaws
to grab prey.

Clouded leopards quietly

sneak up on prey.

These hungry cats

eat deer, monkeys,

and birds.

Clouded Leopard Life Cycle

Females usually give birth
to one to four cubs each year.
As adults, these cats
most likely live alone.

In the wild it is hard to find

clouded leopards.

They are endangered cats.

To save them, zoos are

trying to safely raise cubs.

Glossary

cub—a young clouded leopard

endangered—in danger of dying out

fang—a long, pointed tooth

jaw—a part of the mouth used to grab, bite, and chew

pounce—to jump on something suddenly and grab it

prey—an animal hunted by another animal for food

wilderness—an area of wild land where no people live, such as a dense forest

Read More

Marks, Jennifer L. *Jaguars.* Wildcats. Mankato, Minn.: Capstone Press, 2011.

Pitts, Zachary. *The Pebble First Guide to Wildcats.* Pebble First Guides. Mankato, Minn.: Capstone Press, 2009.

Internet Sites

FactHound offers a safe, fun way to find Internet sites related to this book. All of the sites on FactHound have been researched by our staff.

Here's all you do:

Visit *www.facthound.com*

FactHound will fetch the best sites for you!

Index

Word Count: 165
Grade: 1
Early-Intervention Level: 17